PENNSYLVANIA
Past and Present

Heather Hasan

rosen publishing's
rosen
central®

New York

To my daughter, Sarah Elizabeth, Pennsylvania born and precious

Published in 2010 by The Rosen Publishing Group, Inc.
29 East 21st Street, New York, NY 10010

First Edition

Library of Congress Cataloging-in-Publication Data

Hasan, Heather.
Pennsylvania: past and present / Heather Hasan.—1st ed.
    p. cm.—(The United States: past and present)
Includes bibliographical references and index.
ISBN-13: 978-1-4358-5291-4 (library binding)
ISBN-13: 978-1-4358-5580-9 (pbk)
ISBN-13: 978-1-4358-5581-6 (6 pack)
1. Pennsylvania—Juvenile literature. I. Title.
F149.3.H38 2010
974.8—dc22

2008054214

Manufactured in the United States of America

On the cover: Top left: Independence Hall in Philadelphia. Top right: Pennsylvania Dutch farm in Lancaster County. Bottom: View of downtown Pittsburgh.

Contents

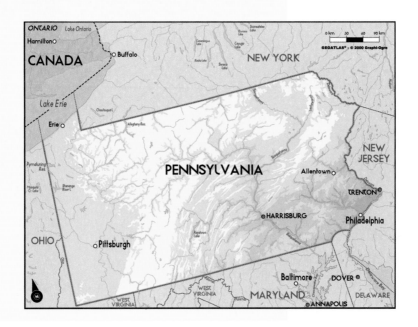

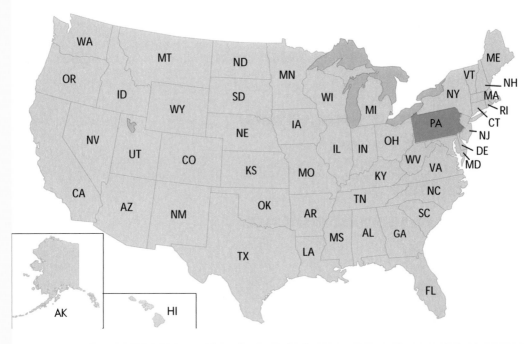

Pennsylvania is located in the northeastern part of the United States *(bottom)*. The state is bordered by New York, New Jersey, Delaware, Maryland, West Virginia, Ohio, and Lake Erie *(top)*.

Introduction

A keystone is the central stone in an arch that holds all the other stones in place. Without it, all of the stones would come crashing down. Pennsylvania is called the Keystone State partly because of its central location among America's original thirteen states. Pennsylvania forms a geographic ridge between the northeastern states and the southern states and between the Atlantic sea and the Midwest.

Pennsylvania also played a "key" role in the founding of the United States. It was the first state to abolish slavery, and one of its towns, Gettysburg, was the site of the Civil War's most decisive battle. During the early days of the United States, Pennsylvania was the center of politics and industry. Both the Declaration of Independence and the U.S. Constitution were written within the state's borders. Coal from Pennsylvania's mines lit and warmed its growing cities, and Pennsylvania steel built the nation's railroads, skyscrapers, and heavy machinery. The people who arrived in Pennsylvania to work in its industries helped to give the United States the diverse population that it has today.

In this book, you'll learn more about the geography, the history, the government, the industry, and the people that have shaped Pennsylvania's past and present.

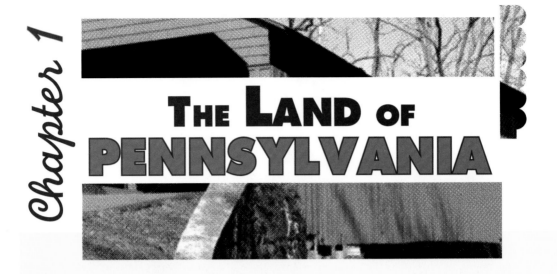

Chapter 1

THE LAND OF PENNSYLVANIA

Pennsylvania is the thirty-third largest state in the United States, covering an area of 46,055 square miles (119,282 square kilometers). To the north and northeast, it is bordered by New York. Across the Delaware River to the east, Pennsylvania is bordered by New Jersey. On the south, Pennsylvania is bordered by Delaware, Maryland, and West Virginia, and to the west lies Ohio. The state is also bordered by Lake Erie, to the northwest.

Pennsylvania's Mountains and Plateaus

Pennsylvania is almost totally covered by mountains. Most of the state is a series of rolling hills, plateaus, ridges, and valleys. The highest point in Pennsylvania is Mount Davis, at 3,213 feet (979 meters) above sea level. The Appalachian Mountains slice through Pennsylvania from the northeastern corner of the state through the south-central part. The section of the Appalachian Mountains that runs through this part of Pennsylvania is called the Ridge and Valley Province. The ridges of the Appalachian Mountains line up one after another, with an average height of between 800 and 1,000 feet (244 and 305 m). A major part of the Ridge and Valley Province is the Great Valley, which stretches from New York to Georgia. The portion of the Great Valley that runs through Pennsylvania is known by several names: the Lebanon Valley, the Cumberland Valley, and the Lehigh Valley. The Appalachian Trail, which runs through the Appalachian Mountains, is popular with hikers. Blue Mountain is a ridge that runs for 150 miles (241 kilometers) and forms the eastern edge of the Appalachian Mountain range. In the northeast corner of Pennsylvania lies 2,400 square miles (6,216 sq km) of a mountainous region called the Pocono Mountains.

Bridal Veil Falls is one of several picturesque waterfalls located in Pennsylvania's Pocono Mountains.

The Allegheny Plateau covers a large part of the northern and western parts of Pennsylvania. In fact, it covers more than half the area of the state. A plateau is a raised area of land with a relatively level top. The Allegheny Plateau is not flat and boring, though. It has a rocky terrain, thick forests, and cascading streams. The Allegheny

Pennsylvania's Wildlife

When settlers arrived in Pennsylvania, the wildlife was plentiful. But the wildlife in the state began to be depleted almost as soon as European colonists arrived. Whereas Native Americans used almost all of the parts of the animals they hunted, European settlers often killed animals for their hides only, which were valuable in the fur trade. At one time, the population of the white-tailed deer (the state animal) was greatly depleted. The bison, the moose, the timber wolf, the black bear, the lynx, and the elk have been hunted to near extinction.

In addition to overhunting, loss of habitat has led to the depletion of the wildlife in Pennsylvania. Starting in colonial days, forests were cleared to make room for farms and to provide lumber. Industry and growing cities have destroyed wetlands, forests, and grasslands. These threats have endangered such local species as the bald eagle, the bog turtle, and the Indian bat. Fortunately, Pennsylvania still has an abundance of wildlife. Thanks to regulated hunting and habitat conservation measures, white-tailed deer and black bear are once again numerous in Pennsylvania.

Plateau is part of the Appalachian Mountain system and is sometimes called the Appalachian Plateau. The eastern edge of the plateau is lined by the Allegheny Mountains. Another plateau, the Piedmont Plateau, occupies the extreme southeastern part of Pennsylvania. The Piedmont region has some of the best farmland in the nation.

The Forests of Pennsylvania

Pennsylvania lies in a large area in the eastern United States that is known as the Appalachian Highlands. The Appalachian Highlands has some of the most densely forested areas in the country. There are about 2 million acres (809,371 hectares) of forestland in the state of Pennsylvania. In fact, about 60 percent of Pennsylvania is forested. In some isolated areas of the state, the forests have remained almost primitive. Pennsylvania's Bureau of Forestry protects sixty-one natural and fourteen wilderness areas in the state. The Allegheny National Forest is found in the northern section of the Allegheny Plateau. This forest provides both recreation and natural beauty.

The eastern hemlock is Pennsylvania's state tree. It has flat needles and is identified as an evergreen tree, since it remains green year-round.

The most common trees in Pennsylvania are the maple, elm, birch, beech, pine, oak, sycamore, and hemlock. The eastern hemlock is Pennsylvania's state tree. Berries and shrubs are abundant in the forests of Pennsylvania. Blackberries, wild cherries, blueberries, raspberries, huckleberries, wild ginger, and wild mint are found throughout Pennsylvania's forests and meadows.

The Delaware River cuts through the Appalachian Mountains to form the Delaware Water Gap. The "gateposts" of the gap are Mt. Minsi, in Pennsylvania, and Mt. Tammany in New Jersey.

Pennsylvania's Waterways

More than 4,500 rivers and streams crisscross Pennsylvania. In fact, it has more deep and useful rivers than any other state. The Susquehanna River cuts through the eastern part of Pennsylvania and flows down to the Chesapeake Bay in Maryland. The Delaware River flows along the eastern edge of the state, forming a border between Pennsylvania and New Jersey and New York. The Delaware River carved a deep gorge through the Appalachian Mountains near

Stroudsburg, called the Delaware Water Gap. In western Pennsylvania, the Allegheny River flows through rolling farmland and low mountains. It joins with the Monongahela River at Pittsburgh to form the Ohio River. This river eventually empties into the Mississippi River.

There are more than three hundred lakes in Pennsylvania. However, few of these are natural lakes. Man-made lakes are formed when people build dams across rivers, flooding the valleys. The largest natural lake in Pennsylvania is Conneaut Lake, found in the northwestern part of the state. It covers about 1.5 square miles (3.9 sq km). However, this lake is small compared to Pennsylvania's artificial ones. The largest man-made lake in Pennsylvania is Raystown Lake. It was formed by a dam on the Juniata River in south-central Pennsylvania and covers about 12 square miles (31 sq km).

Chapter 2

THE HISTORY OF PENNSYLVANIA

The first inhabitants of Pennsylvania migrated there from Asia at least fifteen thousand years ago. These Native Americans hunted bear, deer, bison, and other animals. They gathered berries, nuts, fruit, and roots. They also cleared land and planted such crops as beans, corn, and squash. By the 1600s, there were several Native American tribes living in Pennsylvania.

The largest and most powerful nation living in Pennsylvania was the Lenni-Lenape tribe (called the Delaware by the Europeans). The name Lenni-Lenape means "original people." These people lived in small villages along the Delaware River and built structures called longhouses. The Lenni-Lenape men hunted and fished while the women farmed.

Another Native American tribe, the Susquehannocks, lived along the Susquehanna River in central Pennsylvania. They were also known as the Conestoga. They lived in villages and hunted, farmed, and fished. The Susquehannocks, too, lived in longhouses, which had many rooms and sheltered several families together. The Susquehannocks were fierce warriors, often raiding the villages of the tribes along the Chesapeake Bay. They were also active fur traders, conducting business with Swedish and Dutch trappers along the Delaware River. Other Pennsylvania inhabitants included the Shawnee, the Huron, the Monongahela, and the Erie tribes. They lived in the west. By 1790, disease, war, and forced relocation had reduced the number of Native Americans in the area to only about one thousand.

Early European Settlement

The first European to explore the area that is now Pennsylvania was Captain John Smith of Virginia in 1608. The first permanent European settlement in the region was not settled until 1643, when Swedish settlers developed a colony called New Sweden. It was located just south of today's Philadelphia and reached eastward to Wilmington, Delaware. In 1655, the Dutch gained control over the area and called it New Netherland. Dutch dominance ended, however, when English settlers seized control in 1664.

The Quaker Province

William Penn was born into wealth in London on October 24, 1644. Penn became a Quaker, a persecuted religion at that time, and used his wealth to protect his fellow believers. England's King Charles II owed a huge financial debt to Penn's deceased father, Admiral Sir William Penn, and Penn requested that he be given land in the American colonies as repayment. The king granted Penn the territory between the provinces of Maryland and New York. He named the area in honor of his father. Pennsylvania means "Penn's woods." Penn sailed to his new land in 1682, with the idea of founding a colony where people could experience religious freedom. Before Penn left

William Penn's 1682 treaty with the Lenni-Lenape tribe gave the colonists Kensington, Philadelphia. Here, Penn accepts a belt from the tribe's chief as part of the treaty.

England, he wrote a document called *First Frame of Government*. This document gave the colonists some control in how they would be governed.

When he arrived, Penn established the first permanent English settlement and named it Philadelphia, which means "the City of Brotherly Love." Pennsylvania soon became one of the wealthiest and most influential colonies. Immigrants were attracted by the promises of affordable land, religious freedom, and a voice for the people. Many of the ideas from Penn's *First Frame of Government* found their way in the U.S. Constitution.

Pennsylvania and the French and Indian War

All did not go smoothly in Pennsylvania. Part of the land in western Pennsylvania that the English king gave to Penn was still claimed by England's enemy France. Also, as the Pennsylvania colony prospered and grew, the British colonists' relations with the Native Americans worsened. In 1737, the settlers took over much of the Shawnee and Delaware land in what is referred to as the "Walking Purchase." The Walking Purchase granted the colonists land based upon how far a man could walk in a day and a half. The Native Americans expected that the walk would be made by one man, who would rest and eat. Instead, the colonists had several men run relays to mark the amount of land being purchased. In this way, the Native Americans were cheated out of a large piece of land. As a result, the Delaware and Shawnee migrated to western Pennsylvania and Ohio, where they became allies with the French.

When war broke out between Great Britain and France, many Native Americans fought on the side of France. This war, which lasted from 1754 to 1763, is known as the French and Indian War. One of the bloodiest battles of the war took place in Pennsylvania, along the Monongahela River. There, in 1755, the French and the Indians ambushed British and colonial troops led by General Edward Braddock, wounding or killing most of them. The threat to Pennsylvania finally ended in 1758, when General John Forbes took control of France's Fort Duquesne. Forbes renamed the site Pittsburgh, in honor of the British prime minister, William Pitt the Elder. Forbes then built Fort Pitt, the largest structure that the British built in North America. By the end of the French and Indian War, France had lost its claim on all of the land east of the Mississippi River, except for New Orleans.

General George Washington *(center)* and Major General Marquis de Lafayette visit with American troops at Valley Forge during the harsh winter of 1777–78.

Pennsylvania and the Fight for Independence

When the French and Indian War ended in 1763, Britain needed a way to pay for the costs of the war. To raise money, the British began requiring the colonies in America to pay taxes on household items, such as sugar, tea, and printed materials. This angered the colonists, including Pennsylvanians. Many wanted to separate the colonies from Great Britain. In 1774, leaders in the colonies met in Philadelphia to discuss their troubles with the British. This was the First Continental

Congress. When their grievances to England's King George III were ignored, they met again in Philadelphia in May 1775 for the Second Continental Congress. This time, they discussed fighting for independence. On July 4, 1776, the Declaration of Independence was signed in Philadelphia. This document announced the freedom of the colonies from Great Britain. On July 15, 1776, delegates met to write Pennsylvania's first constitution. This constitution was rewritten in 1790 and is much like the constitution that governs the state today.

Many important Revolutionary War battles were fought in Pennsylvania. In the summer of 1777, the British invaded Pennsylvania, sailing up the Chesapeake Bay and defeating George Washington's troops in the Battle of Brandywine. The British then went on to capture Philadelphia. Washington and his troops retreated and spent a very cold winter in Valley Forge, Pennsylvania, with little food or water. Other battles that were fought in Pennsylvania include those at Germantown, Fort Mifflin, and Whitemarsh.

In 1778, France joined the war on the American side, and the British soon retreated from Philadelphia. The war ended in 1783, with a victory for the colonists. In 1787, the colonies' representatives met once again in Philadelphia to draw up a U.S. constitution. The Pennsylvania Assembly sent eight delegates to the convention, including Ben Franklin. On December 12, 1787, Pennsylvania became the second state to ratify, or approve, the Constitution. Philadelphia served as the country's capital from 1790 until 1800, when the capital was moved to Washington, D.C.

Pennsylvania and the Civil War

In 1781, Pennsylvania adopted the Pennsylvania Emancipation Act, which promised the gradual abolition of slavery in the state.

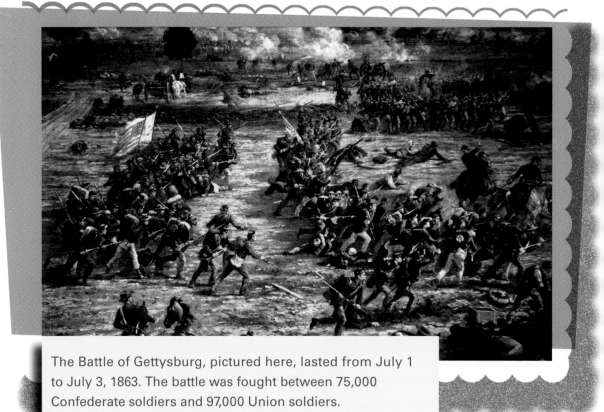

The Battle of Gettysburg, pictured here, lasted from July 1 to July 3, 1863. The battle was fought between 75,000 Confederate soldiers and 97,000 Union soldiers.

Pennsylvania was the first state to forbid slavery. Many in the state helped to free slaves through the Underground Railroad. This was a series of safe homes and hiding places that allowed slaves to safely escape to Canada.

In April 1861, southern states began to secede (leave) the United States over slavery and states' rights. This led to the Civil War (1861–1865), a military conflict between the northern states of America (the Union) and the southern states of America (the Confederacy). The most famous battle of the Civil War, the Battle of Gettysburg, took place in Pennsylvania in 1863. More people died in

Oil in Pennsylvania

In 1859, the world's first commercial oil well was drilled in northwestern Pennsylvania, near the town of Titusville. For the rest of the nineteenth century, Pennsylvania was the nation's top oil producer. The state produced 31 million barrels of oil at its peak in 1891. Oil refineries sprang up throughout the United States to convert crude oil into useful petroleum products. One such product, kerosene, which is used for lighting, was shipped all over the world. Though Pennsylvania is no longer the nation's leading oil producer, its oil reserves are not yet exhausted. In 2002, its oil wells produced about 2.2 million barrels of oil.

this battle than in any other battle fought in North America. The Battle of Gettysburg, which was won by the Union, was considered a turning point in the war. The Gettysburg battlefield cemetery was also the location where Abraham Lincoln gave his famous Gettysburg Address. In all, about 350,000 Pennsylvanians served in the Civil War.

Pennsylvania's Industrial Age

After the Civil War, Pennsylvania developed a strong economy, quickly growing its mining, farming, and manufacturing industries. The state's location on the Eastern Seaboard, its inland waterways, natural resources, and abundance of skilled workers made it ideal for industrial development. Within a few decades, Pennsylvania supplied most of the nation's coal, cement, lumber, and petroleum. Later, it also supplied much of the aluminum and electrical equipment.

This photograph, taken in 1905, shows one of Andrew Carnegie's early steel mills. It was built along the Monongahela River in the town of Braddock, Pennsylvania, in the 1870s.

The mining of iron ore and coal led to the development of Pennsylvania's steel industry. By the late 1800s, steel had taken over as Pennsylvania's leading industry. About 60 percent of the bustling nation's steel was being produced in the steel mills of Pennsylvania. The most prominent steel mills were found in the cities of Bethlehem and Pittsburgh.

Chapter 3

THE GOVERNMENT OF PENNSYLVANIA

Pennsylvania is a commonwealth. Only three other states are official commonwealths: Kentucky, Virginia, and Massachusetts. As in other states, the leaders in a commonwealth are elected by the citizens of the state. In a commonwealth, however, other important officials, such as judges, are also elected by the state's citizens. In other states, the governor often appoints these officials. The idea of a commonwealth existed before the United States was formed, during colonial days.

When William Penn founded the colony of Pennsylvania, he set up a government that would be run by the people, with representatives speaking for them. He also wanted the government to be free from the control of any religion. His ideas were written in an important document called *Penn's Charter*, which became the basis of Pennsylvania's state constitution. Pennsylvania's first constitution was written in 1776, when the colonies declared their independence from England.

From 1682 to 1790, Pennsylvania had a one-house, or unicameral, legislature. A legislature is a lawmaking body. In 1790, a new state constitution established a bicameral legislature, with a house of representatives and a senate. This bicameral legislature has remained to this day. Pennsylvania's legislature adopted new constitutions in 1838, 1874, 1968, and 1999. Pennsylvania's constitution lays out a plan for how the government of the state is run. The specific jobs

In 1701, William Penn wrote the *Charter of Privileges (original shown here)*. This version lasted until the American Revolution, when it was replaced by the state constitution.

within the state government are divided into three groups, or branches: the executive branch, legislative branch, and judicial branch.

The Executive Branch

The executive branch makes sure that laws are enforced. The head of Pennsylvania's executive branch is the governor, who is elected to office by the citizens of the state. According to the Pennsylvania constitution, the governor must be at least thirty years old and a citizen of the United States to be elected. A governor must also have lived in the commonwealth for at least seven years. The governor of Pennsylvania is elected to a four-year term and cannot serve for more than two terms in a row.

The governor is responsible for running the state. He or she represents Pennsylvania when dealing with other states. The governor is in charge of several state departments, including law enforcement, education, agriculture, taxation, and environmental protection. Each department is run by a person whom the governor has appointed. In addition to the governor, there are other executive

Here are Pennsylvania's state flag *(top)* and state seal *(bottom)*. The eagles on both the flag and the seal are symbols of Pennsylvania's sovereignty.

branch officers that are elected by the people. These include the lieutenant governor, the state treasurer, the attorney general, and the auditor general. These officials support the governor in various ways. They may serve an unlimited number of terms, but they may not serve more than two terms in a row.

In Harrisburg, the Capitol Complex is dominated by the domed state capitol building. It also features the Finance Building, Forum Building, and Capitol Park.

The Legislative Branch

Pennsylvania's legislative branch, also known as the General Assembly, creates state laws. It is made up of two parts: the Senate and the House of Representatives. The members of the Senate and the House of Representatives are elected by the people. The Senate has fifty members, each of whom serves four-year terms. The House of Representatives has 203 members. They serve two-year terms.

Laws start out as bills, which are proposed in either the Senate or the House of Representatives. A committee reviews each bill to make

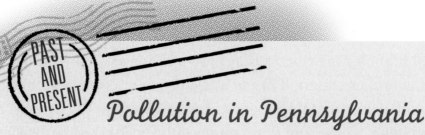

Pollution in Pennsylvania

Donora, Pennsylvania, is a small industrial town that lies on the banks of the Monongahela River, south of Pittsburgh. One night in October 1948, a thick fog hung over Donora. The fog was caused by pollution from the steel mills there. This fog killed twenty people and sickened more than one-third of the town's population of 14,000.

The "Donora Death Fog" helped to convince members of the scientific and medical communities that air pollution can kill people. It eventually led to the Clean Air Act of 1970, which set federal standards to reduce pollution. Pennsylvania developed the Clean Air Act Amendments of 1990, which help to reduce factory air pollution. The state also created the Pennsylvania Land Recycling Program of 1995, which cleans polluted soil and finds new uses for cleaned land.

The Clean Air Act of 1970 placed restrictions on coal burning, which causes acid rain and smog. This led to the decline in Pennsylvania's mining industry. Mining had been a major state industry in Pennsylvania due to its abundant coal resources. Today, however, the coal industry makes up less than 1 percent of Pennsylvania's economy.

sure that it would benefit the people. Once the committee approves the bill, it is brought up for a vote. In order for a bill to become a law, the majority of both sections of the General Assembly must pass it. Once the Senate and House have voted on a bill, it is sent to the governor. When the governor signs a bill, it becomes a law. The governor can veto a bill, or refuse to sign it. If this happens, the General Assembly may override the governor's veto and pass the bill anyway. This can be done only if two out of every three members of both parts of the General Assembly vote in favor of the bill.

The Judicial Branch

The judicial branch makes sure that laws are fair and determines if someone has broken them. This is done in court. Members of the judicial branch select people to serve on a court's jury—the group of citizens that hears a case and determines guilt or innocence. Judges supervise the trials, instruct the jury, and pronounce sentences.

The Supreme Court of Pennsylvania is the oldest court in North America, dating back to 1722. Below it are the two appellate courts, a superior court, and a commonwealth court. These are known as the intermediate appellate courts. These courts hear appeals, or requests to overturn rulings from lower courts. Usually, a case begins in one of Pennsylvania's sixty courts of common pleas. These courts hear lawsuits, which are cases where one person feels that he or she has been wronged by another, as well as criminal cases.

The Supreme Court of Pennsylvania is the final appellate court. It addresses rulings that are appealed from the intermediate appellate courts. It makes sure that the laws in question are in line with the state constitution. The Supreme Court of Pennsylvania is made up of seven judges, called justices, who are elected by the people. They serve ten-year terms. After ten years, they can choose to run for election again or step down. The justice who has served the longest is given the honor of becoming the chief justice.

The Local Governments

Pennsylvania's local government is made up of sixty-seven counties. Most of the counties are governed by a board of three county commissioners. They are elected for four-year terms by the people who live there. Below the county level, Pennsylvania is divided into

Here is the interior of the stately Supreme Court, located in Harrisburg. The Supreme Court is the highest court in the Commonwealth of Pennsylvania.

cities, boroughs, and townships. Pennsylvania's cities are governed by mayors and city councils. There are about 970 boroughs in Pennsylvania. Most boroughs are small, urban communities. According to Pennsylvania law, a borough may become a city if it has at least ten thousand people living in it. Pennsylvania's boroughs are governed by mayors and borough councils. There are about 1,550 townships in Pennsylvania. They provide local government for suburban and rural areas. Most townships are governed by either township commissioners or township supervisors.

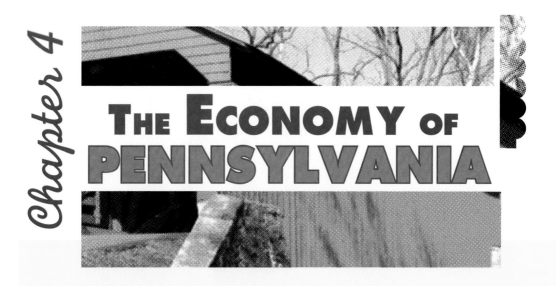

Chapter 4

THE ECONOMY OF PENNSYLVANIA

The ten most populated cities in Pennsylvania are Philadelphia, Pittsburgh, Allentown, Erie, Reading, Scranton, Bethlehem, Lancaster, Altoona, and Harrisburg. The major industrial cities in Pennsylvania are Philadelphia and Pittsburgh. Philadelphia is located in the southeast corner of the state. It is the largest city in Pennsylvania and the fifth-largest city in the United States. Philadelphia is one of the nation's leaders in the financial and insurance industries.

Pittsburgh is located in the southwest corner of Pennsylvania. Because it has roots in the steel industry, Pittsburgh is often called Steel City. In addition to being a steel town, the city has expanded to include such industries as computer technology, printing, and oil refining. Pittsburgh is also known for its health care, its scientific research, and its higher education. Among the many distinguished universities found in Pittsburgh are Carnegie Mellon University, the University of Pittsburgh, and Duquesne University.

The Service Industry

More than one-third of Pennsylvanians work in service-related jobs in industries like health care, banking, and retail sales. Retail sales have always been important in Pennsylvania. The first department store in the United States opened in Philadelphia in 1876. Woolworth's, the first successful dime store, was opened in Lancaster, Pennsylvania. Today, the retail industry is the third most important service industry in Pennsylvania.

The most important service-related jobs in Pennsylvania are social and personal services. These include jobs in places like hospitals, hotels, and law firms. The second most important group of service

Here is the Pittsburgh skyline, as seen from the West End Overlook.

jobs in Pennsylvania are jobs in places like real estate companies, insurance companies, and banks. Other important service-related jobs are those in transportation, communication, and government.

Tourism

Pennsylvania is rich in history, and there are many historic sites for visitors to enjoy. In fact, Pennsylvania ranks sixth in the nation in tourism. Tourists are drawn to Philadelphia's Independence National Historical Park. This park preserves more than twenty sites that are associated with the early history of the United States and the time

Visitors learn about the Liberty Bell in Philadelphia. The bell bears the inscription, "Proclaim LIBERTY throughout all the Land unto all the inhabitants thereof."

that Philadelphia served as the U.S. capital (1790–1800). Here, tourists can visit Independence Hall, where both the Declaration of Independence and the Constitution of the United States were written. Visitors can also view the familiar cracked Liberty Bell, which was rung on July 8, 1776, to celebrate the Declaration of Independence. They can also visit the home of Benjamin Franklin (1706–1790), the great American statesman and inventor.

Pennsylvania was the site of many important battles that shaped our nation. Tourists can visit the Gettysburg National Military Park, where the Battle of Gettysburg took place (July 1–3, 1863). Other battlefields from the French and Indian War (1754–1763), the War of 1812 (1812–1815), the American Revolution (1775–1783), and the Civil War (1861–1865) have also been preserved or restored for visitors.

Pennsylvania is also great for museum lovers. One of the world's finest art museums, the Philadelphia Museum of Art, is located in Philadelphia. The Rodin Museum is also found there. For those who like science, the Franklin Institute in Philadelphia is one of the best. In Pittsburgh, the Carnegie Institute houses many famous paintings. The Farm Museum, near Lancaster, and the William Penn Memorial Museum in Harrisburg both house historical wonders.

The Pennsylvania Dutch region, in south-central Pennsylvania, is a favorite among tourists. Here, the Old Order Amish, the Old Order Mennonites, and other plain sects have retained their traditional customs and dress. They still farm with horses and oxen, and use horses and buggies for transportation.

Pennsylvania's natural beauty is another draw for visitors. The state has a full array of popular vacation spots. Tourists go to Lake Erie to enjoy summer water sports as well as the sandy beaches and dunes. In the east, visitors to the Pocono Mountains enjoy golfing, fishing, hunting, hiking, and skiing. In the Allegheny National Forest, tourists can enjoy the beauty of the state as they hike past hillsides covered with flowers.

Tourists to Lancaster County can visit the area and see horse-drawn buggies *(above)* or sit down to dinner with an Amish family.

The Manufacturing Industry

Pennsylvania is one of the nation's leading manufacturing states. About two out of every ten workers in Pennsylvania work in the manufacturing business. Today, the major manufacturing industries in Pennsylvania include the production of food, chemicals, metals, industrial machinery, and electronic equipment, along with printing and publishing.

Pennsylvania's most important product is food. Some of its best-known food products are crackers, sausage, bread, and canned mushrooms. Pennsylvania is a great place for snack lovers. It has food-processing plants that produce cookies, cakes, chocolate, ice cream, pretzels, and potato chips. The H. J. Heinz Corporation in Pittsburgh makes sauces, soups, pickles, and ketchup. The state's Hershey factory is the world's largest manufacturer of chocolate and cocoa products.

Chemical production is important in Pennsylvania, and the state is one of the top producers of pharmaceuticals. The Philadelphia area has some of the biggest drug companies in the country. It is also home to research laboratories and medical schools. In fact, there is a stretch of road just outside of Philadelphia that is called the Medical Mile. Other chemicals produced in Pennsylvania are used in the production of petroleum, paints, and resins.

The Agricultural Industry

Pennsylvania has about fifty thousand farms, which cover about one-third of the state. Most of the farmland of Pennsylvania is found in the southeast (the Piedmont region) and in the Great Appalachian Valley. Pennsylvania also has the largest rural population in the

PAST AND PRESENT

The Steel Industry in Pennsylvania

In the 1870s, Andrew Carnegie brought steel manufacturing to Pennsylvania. He set up steel mills near Pittsburgh in the towns of Braddock and Homestead. He started the Carnegie Steel Company and joined with other steel mills to form the U.S. Steel Corporation. By the 1900s, U.S. Steel and another company in Pennsylvania, Bethlehem Steel, were producing most of the steel in the United States. The United States was the largest and lowest-cost producer of steel in the world. Steel from Pennsylvania built the George Washington Bridge, the Brooklyn Bridge, the Chrysler Building, and the Empire State Building.

The steel industry did well until the 1960s, when U.S. companies could no longer compete with low-cost steel being produced by other countries, such as Japan. By the 1970s, a third of Pennsylvania's steel workers were jobless. This brought economic hardship to Pennsylvania. The state responded by encouraging other industries, such as electronics and computer companies, to move there. Today, high-technology industries are growing fast—and Pennsylvania still produces more specialty steel than any other U.S. state.

United States. Livestock and livestock products, such as milk, account for about 70 percent of Pennsylvania's farm income. Milk is Pennsylvania's leading agricultural product, produced mainly on farms in eastern Pennsylvania.

Cattle, used for meat, is the state's second most important agricultural product. Most cattle are raised along the Susquehanna River in the southeastern part of Pennsylvania, an area that also has many poultry and egg farms.

Pennsylvania is home to a mixture of large and small dairy farms. This dairy farm is located in the central Pennsylvania mountains.

Pennsylvania is the largest mushroom producer in the nation. The state also produces corn and hay, which are mainly used to feed cattle. Other crops grown in Pennsylvania include potatoes, oats, wheat, and soybeans. Pennsylvania also produces fruits. Apples, cherries, and peaches are grown in the southern part of the state. Grapes are grown in the Erie lowlands of the northwest.

Chapter 5

PEOPLE FROM PENNSYLVANIA: PAST AND PRESENT

The Keystone State has been home to many well-known figures throughout history. This chapter offers a varied sampling of Pennsylvania's famous sons and daughters, from politicians and industrialists to artists, authors, and educators.

Benjamin Franklin (1706–1790) Although he was born in Boston, Benjamin Franklin made his life in Philadelphia and became one of colonial Pennsylvania's most famous citizens. Franklin founded the first library, insurance company, and fire department in America. He was a publisher, a printer, a scientist, an author, an inventor, and a statesman. Franklin signed the Declaration of Independence and was largely responsible for convincing the French to aid the colonies during the American Revolution.

Henry John Heinz (1844–1919) Henry J. Heinz was a German American businessman. In 1876, Heinz founded the F & J Heinz Company. One of the company's first products was tomato ketchup. Heinz also produced such products as pickled cucumbers, sauerkraut, celery sauce, vinegar, pickles, and jellies. By 1896, Heinz was known as the "Pickle King."

On *Mr. Rogers' Neighborhood,* Fred Rogers started every show by switching his suit coat and dress shoes for a sweater and tennis shoes.

Fred Rogers (1928–2003) Fred McFeely Rogers was born in Latrobe, Pennsylvania, in 1928. Rogers was known as Mr. Rogers, a character on the children's television show *Mister Rogers' Neighborhood*, which he created in 1966. With his soft-spoken manner and whimsical songs, Rogers educated and entertained children for more than three decades. In 1999, he was inducted into the Television Hall of Fame. In 2002, Rogers received the Presidential Medal of Freedom, the nation's highest civilian honor.

Betsy Ross (1752–1836) Betsy Ross was a seamstress born in Philadelphia as Elizabeth Griscom. Many people believe that she made the first American flag. According to legend, in June 1776, George Washington and two associates called upon Ross to ask her to sew the flag. They gave her a sketch with six-pointed stars, but Ross insisted on five. Whether or not the story is true, Ross is treasured in American tradition

Sports in Pennsylvania

Pennsylvania has come a long way since William Penn had his first colonial legislature ban the "riotous sports" he feared would tempt his colonists to immoral behavior. Today, there are seven major professional sports teams in Pennsylvania. In Philadelphia, the teams are the Phillies (baseball), the Flyers (hockey), the 76ers (basketball), and the Eagles (football). In Pittsburgh, the teams are the Pirates (baseball), the Penguins (hockey), and the Steelers (football).

Interestingly, there was once a football team in Pennsylvania called the Steagles. This team, which existed in 1943, was a combination of the Pittsburgh Steelers and the Philadelphia Eagles. The Steagles were a result of World War II. During the war, all of the healthy men were away fighting, and money that was normally used for professional sports was instead used to support the war effort. In order to ensure the survival of both teams during these tough times, they were combined into a single Pennsylvania team. Today, the teams are separate once more and are both hugely popular.

as the seamstress of the first American flag. Ross's house in Philadelphia is a popular site for tourists.

Louisa May Alcott (1832–1888) Louisa May Alcott was a writer born in Germantown, Pennsylvania. Before she began writing novels, Alcott was the editor of a children's magazine, *Merry's Museum*. She is famous for her children's novel *Little Women*, which she published in 1868 to the delight of little girls all over the world. Some of Alcott's other well-known books include *An Old-Fashioned Girl* (1870), *Little Men* (1871), and *Jo's Boys* (1886).

James Buchanan (1791–1868) Born near Mercersburg, James Buchanan is the only U.S. president to hail from Pennsylvania. Buchanan was elected to the Pennsylvania legislature in 1814 and later represented the state for ten years in the U.S. Congress. Buchanan then served as minister to both Russia and England, as a U.S. senator, and as secretary of state. In 1856, Buchanan was elected the fifteenth president of the United States. As of 2009, he is the only U.S. president who never married.

Reggie Jackson (1946–) Reginald Martinez Jackson was born in Wyncote, Pennsylvania. He gained recognition as a power hitter beginning in 1969, when he cracked forty-seven home runs for the Oakland A's. Jackson later led the New York Yankees to two World Series championships, in 1977 and 1978. During games 5 and 6 of the 1977 World Series, Jackson hit four consecutive home runs, each off of the first pitch of four different Los Angeles Dodgers pitchers. For this, he was nicknamed "Mr. October." Jackson retired from baseball in 1987 and was inducted into the Baseball Hall of Fame in 1993.

Andrew Carnegie (1835–1919) Andrew Carnegie was the major figure in Pennsylvania's steel industry. He was born in Scotland in 1835 but came to the United States at the age of thirteen. Carnegie began to build steel mills in Pennsylvania in the early 1870s and became one of the wealthiest men in the world. He wanted to help society with his fortune, so he created the Carnegie Foundation. Through his foundation, Carnegie built 2,500 public libraries across the United States and gave more than $350 million to charities. He is quoted as saying, "He who dies rich, dies disgraced."

Bill Cosby (1937–)
William Henry (Bill) Cosby Jr. was born in Philadelphia, Pennsylvania, in 1937. Cosby started working as a stand-up comedian while he attended college at Temple University in Philadelphia. In his lifetime, he has been successful onstage, on television, and in the movies. Cosby is best known for his hit TV comedy *The Cosby Show*, which aired from 1984 to 1992. Cosby has been a generous contributor to education and the arts.

Andrew Carnegie started out poor, but he became one of the richest individuals of his era by building the American steel industry.

Milton S. Hershey (1857–1945) Milton Snavely Hershey was born in Derry Church, Pennsylvania. In 1903, Hershey

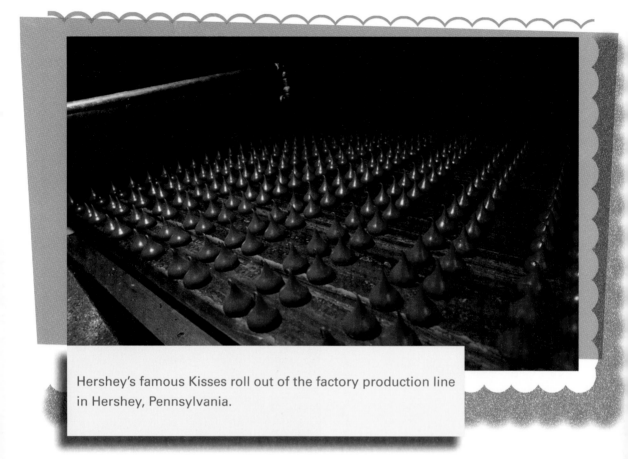

Hershey's famous Kisses roll out of the factory production line in Hershey, Pennsylvania.

built a chocolate factory in his hometown. In fact, he built an entire town, which was later named Hershey. Like Andrew Carnegie, Hershey was a great philanthropist. In 1909, he started the Hershey Industrial School (later renamed the Milton Hershey School), a home and school for orphans. The Hershey Company remains one of the top manufacturers of chocolate today. The Hershey Museum and the Hershey Park amusement park are popular tourist attractions.

Timeline

1608	Captain John Smith arrives in Pennsylvania.
1638	Swedish fur traders form the first European colony near present-day Philadelphia.
1682	William Penn arrives in Pennsylvania.
1685	Philadelphia becomes the capital of Pennsylvania.
1755	The French and Indians defeat the British and the colonists in the battle at Fort Duquesne on the Monongahela River.
1759	Coal is discovered near Pittsburgh.
1776	The Declaration of Independence is signed in Philadelphia, Pennsylvania.
1777	General George Washington and his troops are defeated by the British at the Battle of Brandywine; the British capture Philadelphia.
1778	The British retreat from Philadelphia.
1781	Pennsylvania passes the first law in the United States abolishing slavery.
1787	The Constitutional Convention meets in Philadelphia and drafts the U.S. Constitution. Pennsylvania is the second state to ratify it.
1790–1800	Philadelphia is the capital of the United States.
1863	The bloodiest battle of the Civil War takes place in Gettysburg, Pennsylvania.
1873	Andrew Carnegie begins the large-scale production of iron and steel.
1970	The Clean Air Act is passed; Pennsylvania's coal industry is affected.
1979	Worst civilian nuclear accident in U.S. history occurs when a nuclear reactor melts down at Three Mile Island, near Harrisburg.
2001	Hijacked United Airlines Flight 93 crashes in a field in Somerset County, Pennsylvania, killing all forty-four people aboard.
2009	The Pittsburgh Steelers win a record sixth Superbowl championship.

Pennsylvania at a Glance

Year of statehood	December 12, 1878 (the second state)
Area	45,308 square miles (117,348 sq km); 33rd among the states
Highest elevation	Mount Davis—3,213 feet (979 m) above sea level
Lowest elevation	Sea level, along the Delaware River in southeast Pennsylvania
Population	12,281,054 (6th most populous state)
Capital	Harrisburg (former capitals: Philadelphia and Lancaster)
Most populated city	Philadelphia
State song	"Pennsylvania"
State bird	Ruffed grouse (*Bonasa umbellus*)
State tree	Eastern hemlock (*Tsuga canadensis*)
State insect	Pennsylvania firefly (*Photuris Pennsylvanica*)
State flower	Mountain laurel (*Kalmia latifolia*)
State motto	"Virtue, Liberty, and Independence"
State nickname	"The Keystone State"

State Flag

State Seal

Major rivers	Delaware, Monongahela, Allegheny, Susquehanna, Ohio, Schuylkill, Lehigh, Juniata, Lackawanna
Major mountain chains	Appalachian, Pocono, Allegheny
State fish	Brook trout (*Salvelinus fontinalis*)
Chief agricultural products	Milk, livestock, poultry, eggs, mushrooms, potatoes, oats soybeans, apples, cherries, peaches, grapes, maple syrup
Major industries	Manufacturing, service, tourism, medical research and pharmaceuticals, oil refining
Origin of state name	Pennsylvania means "Penn's woods." It was named in honor of Admiral William Penn

State Bird

State Flower

GLOSSARY

agriculture Occupation or business of farming and animal husbandry.

deplete To drain or lessen in quantity, number, or value.

economy Way people use and produce goods; how people make money.

endangered At risk of becoming extinct.

executive branch Group that runs a state or government.

extinction The condition of no longer being or existing.

habitat Natural environment of an animal.

industry Organizations and businesses that add to the economy.

judicial branch Judges and the courts.

legislative branch Part of government that makes laws.

manufacturing Industry that makes a product.

plateau Raised area of land with a relatively level top.

province Part of a county or colony.

Quaker Member of the Society of Friends, a Christian denomination that was founded in England in the seventeenth century. Quakers are committed to peaceful resolutions to conflicts.

Revolutionary War War that the colonists fought with Great Britain to free themselves from British rule.

rural Related to the country or country people.

settlement Place that has just recently been populated.

tax Money paid to the government

FOR MORE INFORMATION

Gettysburg National Military Park

1195 Baltimore Pike, Suite 100

Gettysburg, PA 17325

(717) 334-1124, ext. 8023

Web site: http://www.nps.gov/gett/index.htm

The Gettysburg National Military Park provides programs and historical education about the Battle of Gettysburg.

Independence National Historical Park

143 South Third Street

Philadelphia, PA 19106

(215) 965-2305

Web site: http://www.nps.gov/index

Independence National Historical Park includes three blocks in the city of Philadelphia. Visitors can learn the rich history of the area.

Pennsylvania Chamber of Business and Industry

417 Walnut Street

Harrisburg, PA 17101

(800) 225-7224

Web site: http://www.pachamber.org

The Pennsylvania Chamber of Business and Industry is the largest broad-based business association in Pennsylvania.

Pennsylvania Historical and Museum Commission (PHMC)

State Museum Building

300 North Street

Harrisburg, PA 17120

(717) 787-3362

Web site: http://www.portal.state.pa.us/portal/server.pt?open=512&mode=2&objID=1426

The PHMC is the official history agency of the Commonwealth of Pennsylvania.

Web Sites

Due to the changing nature of Internet links, Rosen Publishing has developed an online list of Web sites related to the subject of this book. This site is updated regularly. Please use this link to access the list:

http://www.rosenlinks.com/uspp/papp

FOR FURTHER READING

Anderson, Dale. *The American Revolution*. Austin, TX: Raintree Steck-Vaughn Publishers, 2003.

Cole, Michael D. *Three Mile Island: Nuclear Disaster*. Berkeley Heights, NJ: Enslow, 2002.

Coleman, Bill. *The Gift to Be Simple: Life in the Amish Country*. San Francisco, CA: Chronicle Books, 2001.

Cousins, Margaret. *Ben Franklin of Old Philadelphia*. New York, NY: Random House, 2004.

Doherty, Craig A., and Katherine M. Doherty. *Pennsylvania* (Thirteen Colonies) New York, NY: Facts On File, 2005.

Lutz, Norma Jean. *William Penn: Founder of Democracy*. Broomall, PA: Chelsea House, 2000.

Phillips, Margaret Coull. *Pennsylvania: Seeds of a Nation*. Farmington Hills, MI: KidHaven Press, 2003.

Prentzas, G. S. *A Primary Source History of the Colony of Pennsylvania*. New York, NY: The Rosen Publishing Group, 2006.

Weiner, Roberta, and James R. Arnold. *Pennsylvania: The History of Pennsylvania Colony, 1681–1776*. Chicago, IL: Raintree Publishers, 2005.

BIBLIOGRAPHY

Capo, Fran, and Scott Bruce. *It Happened in Pennsylvania*. Guilford, CT: The Globe Pequot Press, 2005.

DeFord, Deborah H. *Pennsylvania: Life in the Thirteen Colonies*. New York, NY: Children's Press, 2004.

Hinman, Bonnie. *Pennsylvania: William Penn and the City of Brotherly Love*. Hockessin, DE: Mitchell Lane Publishers, 2006.

Ingram, Scott. *Pennsylvania: The Keystone State*. Milwaukee, WI: World Almanac Library, 2002.

Krass, Peter. *Carnegie*. New York, NY: John Wiley & Sons, 2002.

O'Connell, Kim A. *Pennsylvania: A MyReportLinks.com Book*. Berkeley Heights, NJ: Enslow Publishers, 2003.

Sherrow, Victoria. *Pennsylvania*. Farmington Hills, MI: Lucent Books, 2001.

Somervill, Barbara A. *Pennsylvania: From Sea to Shining Sea*. New York, NY: Children's Press, 2003.

INDEX

About the Author

Heather Elizabeth Hasan was born and raised in the great state of Pennsylvania. In fact, she is a sixth-generation Pennsylvanian. She grew up hearing stories about Pennsylvania from her grandmother, Elizabeth James. Hasan currently lives in the Poconos of Pennsylvania with her husband, Omar; their sons, Samuel and Matthew; and their daughter, Sarah.

Photo Credits

Cover (top left), pp. 24, 34 Shutterstock.com; cover (top right) Michael Townsend/ Getty Images; cover (bottom) © www.istockphoto.com/Sharon Dominick; pp. 3, 6, 12, 21, 28, 35, 41 © www.istockphoto.com/Dobresum; p. 4 (top) © GeoAtlas; p. 7 © W. Cody/Corbis; p. 9 © Martin B. Withers; Frank Lane Picture Agency/Corbis; p. 10 © Bob Krist/Corbis; p. 14 Stock Montage/Hulton Archive/Getty Images; p. 16 Art Resource, NY; p. 18 MPI/Hulton Archive/Getty Images; p. 20 © Corbis; p. 22 American Philosophical Society; pp. 23 (top), 42 (left) Courtesy of Robesus, Inc.; p. 27 © Richard Cummins/SuperStock; p. 29 © www.istockphoto.com/Jeremy Edwards; p. 30 Don Murray/Getty Images; p. 31 Stan Honda/AFP/Getty Images; p. 36 © AP Images; p. 39 Library of Congress Prints and Photographs Division; p. 40 © Richard T. Nowitz/Corbis; p. 43 (left) Wikimeida Commons; p. 43 (right) Wikimedia Commons from www.biolib.de.

Designer: Les Kanturek; Editor: Christopher Roberts;
Photo Researcher: Cindy Reiman